THe Calm COLORING BOOK

THE
Calm
COLORING
BOOK

LOVELY IMAGES TO SET YOUR IMAGINATION FREE

THUNDER BAY
P · R · E · S · S
San Diego, California

THUNDER BAY
P·R·E·S·S

Thunder Bay Press
An imprint of Printers Row Publishing Group
10350 Barnes Canyon Road, Suite 100, San Diego, CA 92121
www.thunderbaybooks.com

Printers Row Publishing Group is a division of Readerlink Distribution Services, LLC.
The Thunder Bay Press name and logo are trademarks of Readerlink Distribution Services, LLC.

All notations of errors or omissions should be addressed to Thunder Bay Press, Editorial Department,
at the above address. All other correspondence (author inquiries, permissions) concerning the
content of this book should be addressed to Arcturus Holdings Limited, 26/27 Bickels Yard, 151-153
Bermondsey Street, London SE1 3HA, info@arcturuspublishing.com.

ISBN: 978-1-62686-625-6
CH004881NT

Cover design: Maki Ryan

Printed in China
20 19 18 17 16 3 4 5 6 7

INTRODUCTION

More and more adults are discovering the stress-busting benefits of coloring. This gentle, focused activity helps to declutter the mind and relax the body, and has the added bonus of providing you with a portfolio of beautiful artwork to keep.

This collection of outlines includes flowers, birds, mandalas, stained-glass windows, and other intricate patterns inspired by nature. The variety and playful style of these images gives you the opportunity to immerse yourself in calm creativity without the added stress of having to start from scratch with a blank sheet of paper.

You can choose your color combinations carefully or pick them at random. Use whatever medium works for you—felt pens, markers, gel pens, pencils, watercolor pencils—it really doesn't matter. As your confidence grows, so will your desire to experiment, and in time you may decide you want to draw and color your own outlines. Whatever you choose to do, have fun!

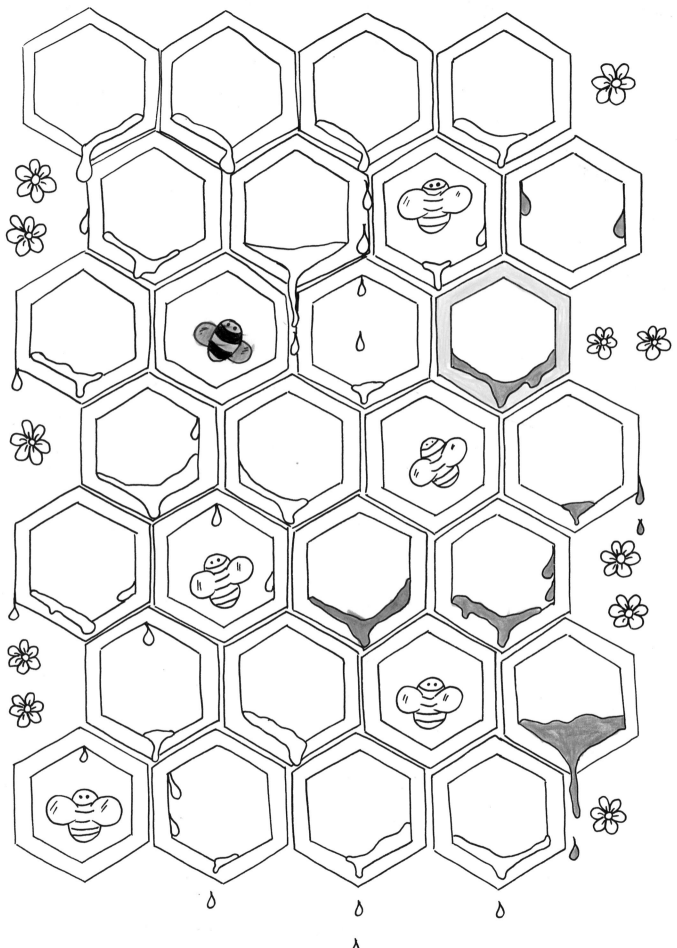

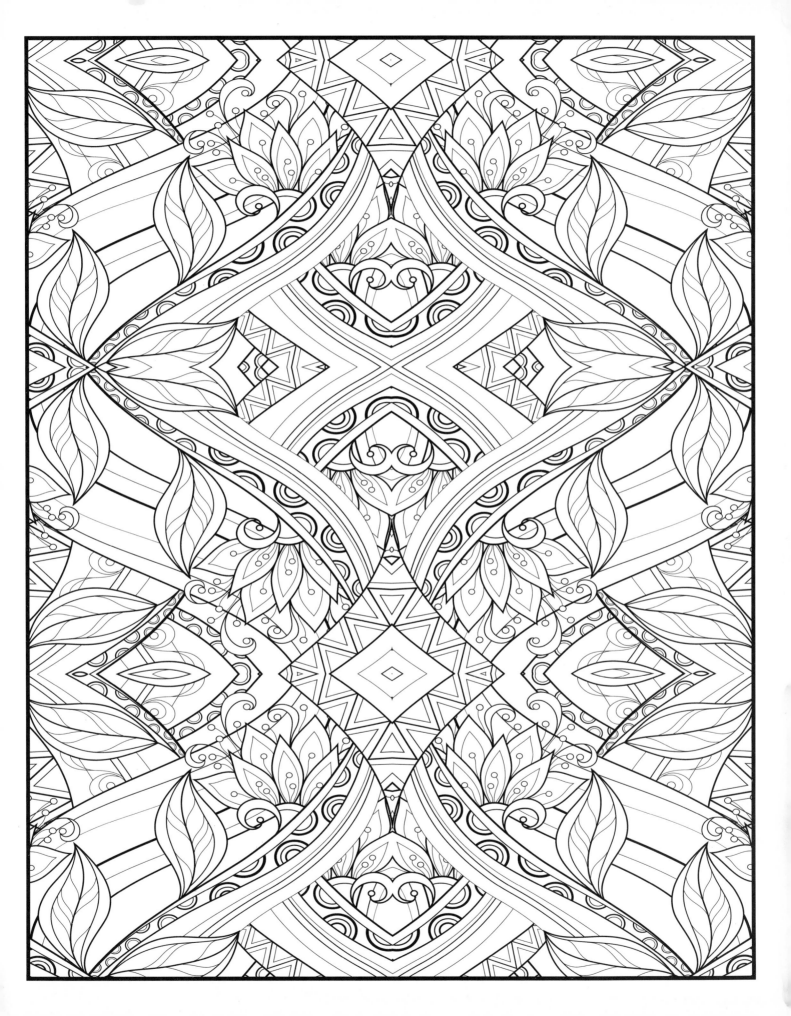

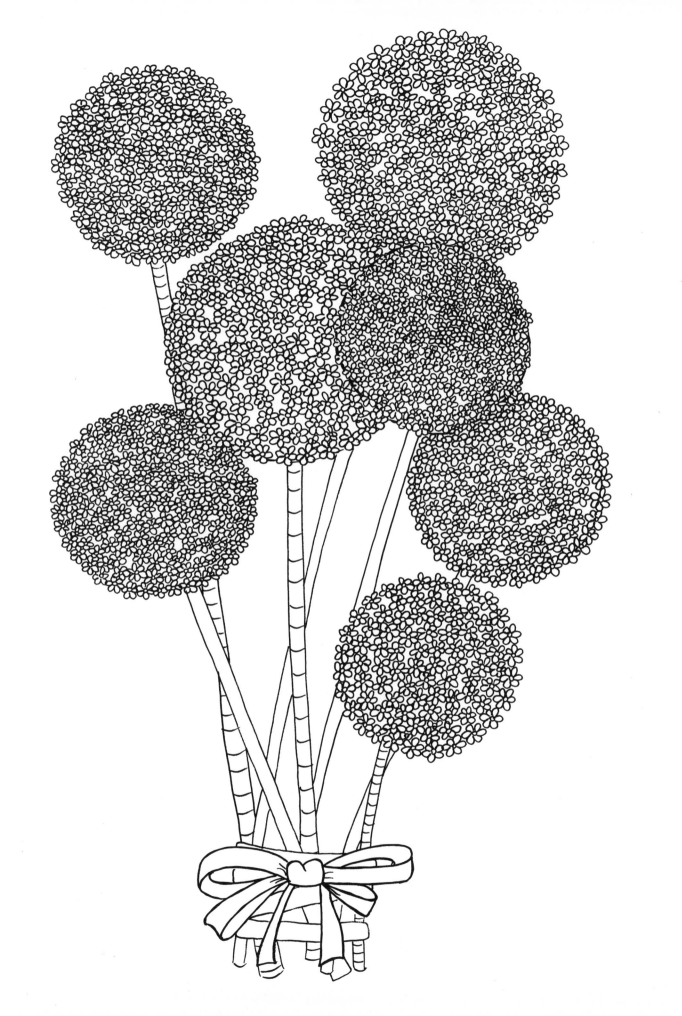

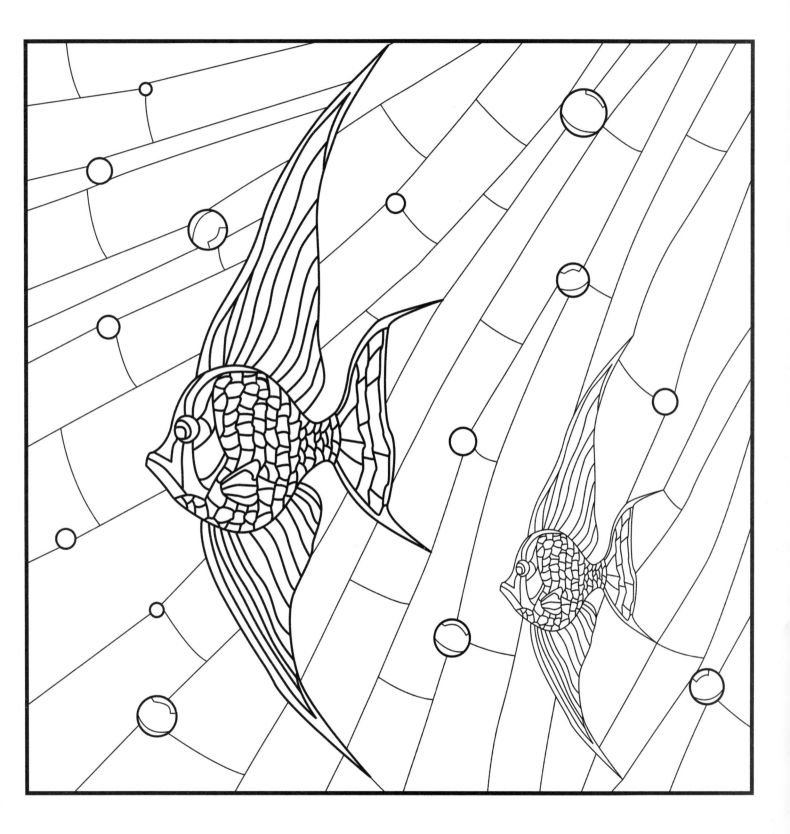

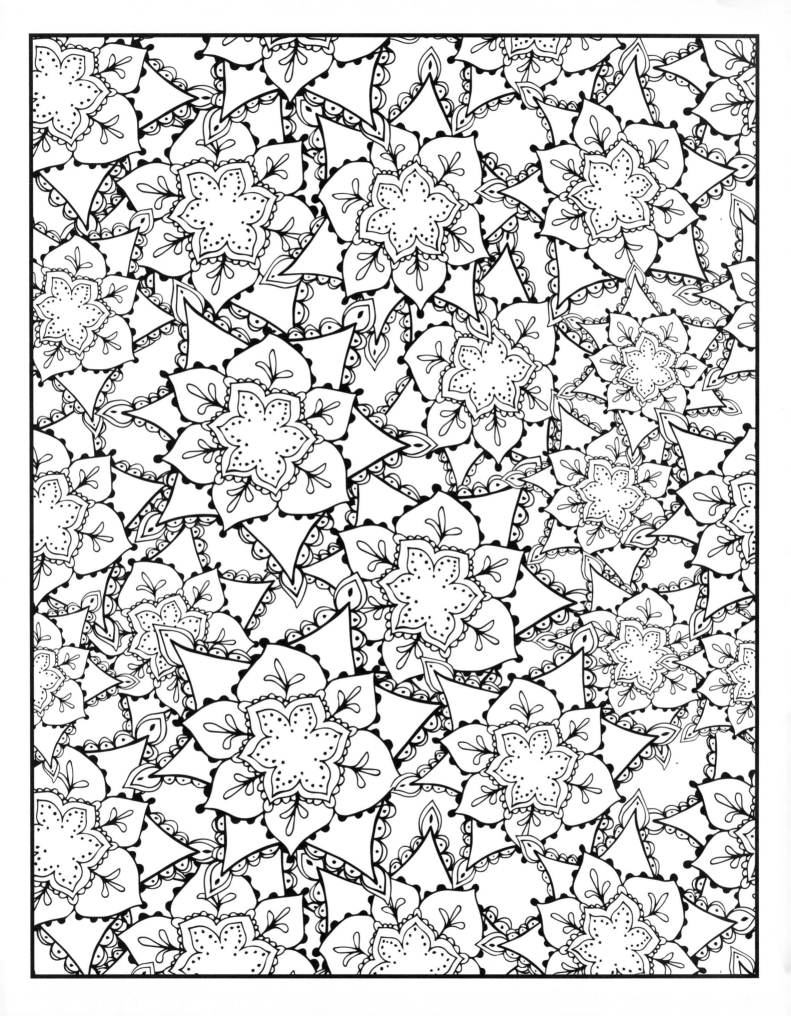

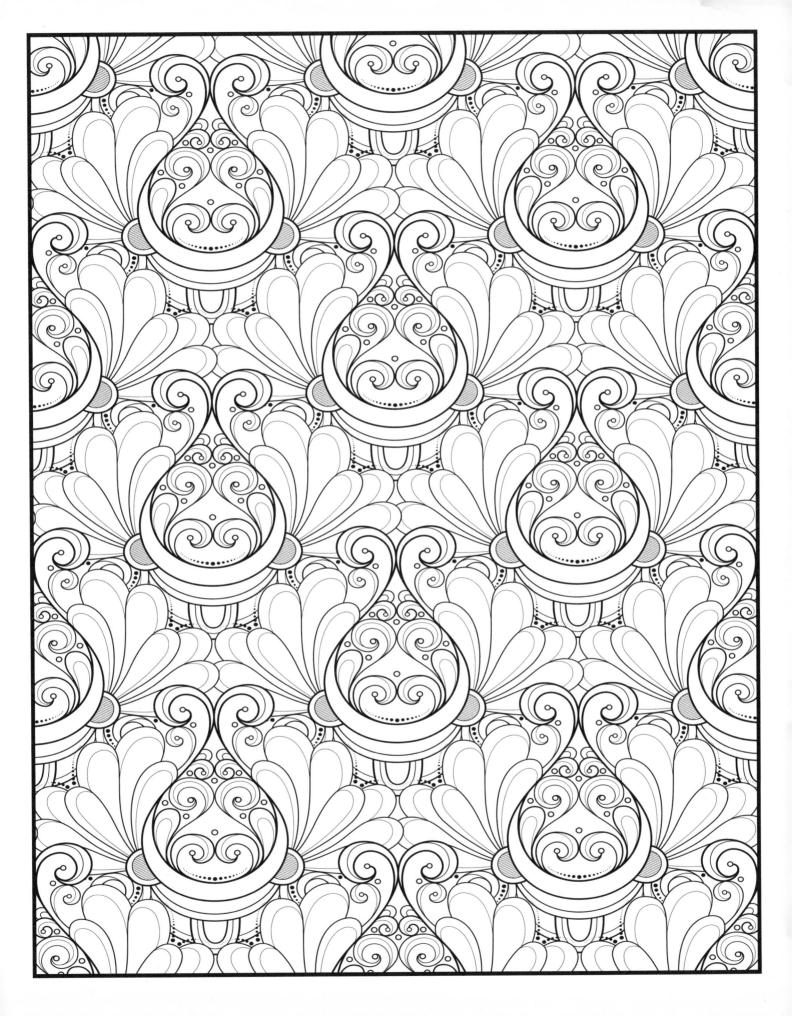